CU00459668

Images in Time

Vol 3

Images in Time

Vol 3

A photographic history
of Orkney's past

from the photographs of
J. W. Sinclair

Compiled by
Norman F. Sinclair

© Norman F. Sinclair

All rights reserved

Published 2000

Published by

The Orcadian Limited

(Kirkwall Press),

Hell's Half Acre, Hatston,

Kirkwall, Orkney,

KW15 1DW

Printed by

The Orcadian Limited

Hell's Half Acre, Hatston,

Kirkwall, Orkney,

KW15 1DW

ISBN 1-902957-10-5

Introduction

Born in Sanday in 1901, Jimmy Sinclair's photographic career spanned more than 60 years, during which time he took an untold number of photographs of Orkney.

From agricultural shows and Ba' winners to royal visits and wartime scenes, Jimmy Sinclair always made sure he was in the right place at the right time to preserve on film the day to day events of the county. Some of those events made their indelible mark in the history books – in 1919 Jimmy, armed with a hand wound movie camera, managed to capture on film the scuttling of the German fleet – a unique reel that was shown in cinemas all over the country. And a few years later he was back in Scapa Flow to record the raising of those same ships by a team of salvage experts.

Jimmy got his first job working in a butcher's shop at the age of 14 before becoming an apprentice baker with the Orkney firm R. Garden Ltd. when he was paid ten shillings a week.

He had his first contact with the world of film when he became assistant projectionist at Orkney's first Electric Theatre. When the head projectionist left, he took over and stayed for six years.

It was at this time that he became interested in still photography and he bought himself his first camera for £6. After setting up a travelling picture show throughout the isles, he took over his first premises in West Castle Street, Kirkwall, before moving to a studio in Castle Street.

He then built himself a wooden studio at School Place before buying property in King Street where he remained until he retired. During most of this time he also ran a shop in Bridge Street where he sold records and musical instruments as well as photographic equipment.

Jimmy Sinclair died on June 8, 1984 when his collection of more than four thousand negatives and prints passed into the hands of his son Norman.

After wading through this mammoth collection, this compilation was put together, not only to celebrate Jimmy Sinclair's career but to provide a fascinating insight into Orkney's past.

The information contained within this book could not have been put together without the tireless efforts of Norman F. Sinclair whose in-depth local knowledge has been invaluable.

Norman has spent immeasurable amounts of time, tracking down people from Orkney and further afield to gather snippets of information, while at the same time stirring people's memories.

MYLES HODNETT
(co-author of Images in Time Vol. 1)

To my Father,
James W. Sinclair

1 – A memorial plaque was gifted to St Magnus Cathedral by the people of Norway to commemorate the 700th anniversary of the death of King Haakon Haakonsson in 1263. The platform party are, left to right: Rev. John M. Rose (minister of the cathedral); Bert Grieve (halberdier); Andrew Buchan (town clerk); Billy Jolly (Norwegian Consul); the Cultural Attaché from the Norwegian Embassy, who unveiled the memorial tablet; Provost James Scott, who accepted the gift on behalf of the town; and Tom Sclater (halberdier). The plaque now lies in St Rognvald's Chapel over the position where the king's body lay before being taken back to Norway.

Following the indecisive Battle of Largs, King Haakon, and what remained of his once great fleet, sought shelter in Scapa Flow. He took up winter quarters for himself in the Bishop's Palace in Kirkwall where he died at Yule in 1263. His body was buried in the Cathedral until the spring of 1264 when it was returned to Norway for burial in Bergen.

2 – Fourteen Post Office engineers received safe driving awards in 1961. The presentations were made by Mr R. C. Birnie, Telephone Manager, Aberdeen, at Telephone House, Old Scapa Road, Kirkwall. Also present was Provost James Scott of Kirkwall. From the left: Johnnie Morrison, John Donaldson, Provost James Scott, Jack Neilson, Mr R. C. Birnie, Sinclair Drever, Brian Roxby, Johnnie Jamieson, Alan Rosie, Jimmy Urquhart, Bob Foubister, not known and George Robinson.

3 – In August, 1962 the new Tower Showroom, Junction Road, Kirkwall was opened by the MP, Jo Grimond, and pictured are some of the general public waiting to inspect the new premises and Ford exhibits. W. R. Tullock and Sons were the local Ford agents and were celebrating 50 years Ford Service with a Golden Jubilee Week.

4 – Inside the new
showroom.

5 – Staff of W. R. Tullock and Sons and their partners pose for a commemorative photograph.

6 – In 1963, for the second year in succession, Catherine Farquhar won the first round of the Miss Interflora Personality Girl competition at Kirkwall. Catherine, Moira Laird (right) and Helen Sinclair (left) are seen here with the judges: Mrs Georgina Leitch (Honorary Treasurer, Kirkwall Town Council), John Gear (Head Postmaster) and Jim Dick (Union of Post Office Workers).

The County Show of 1963 saw a crowd of 7,000 at the Bignold Park, Kirkwall, on a dull, dry day, to inspect for themselves, the best of Orkney's livestock. Many of the exhibits had been prize winners at their own shows during the previous week.

7 – Having already taken top prize at the St Margaret's Hope show, a four-year-old pure-bred A.A. cow, Butora of Kincardine, shown by T. Dearness, Southfield, Burray, became Supreme Champion at the County.

8 – The reserve champion also came from the pure-bred section, the winner being a yearling heifer shown by J. S. Baillie, Sebay, Tankerness.

9 – The champion shorthorn was the previous year's county champion, a seven-year-old roan bull, Easter Lovat Brando, shown by J. W. & A. K. Work, Queenamoan, Sandwick. Two days earlier he had been selected as the West Mainland champion for the second successive year.

10 – The champion of the Shapinsay Show, an 18-month-old cross steer, shown by R. Johnston, Hewan, Shapinsay, won the cup for the best butcher's beast at the County. It was also reserve cross-bred champion. It was sold at the auction mart the following Monday for £150 to D. G. Spence, Wideford Mains, St Ola.

11 – The overall dairy champion of the 1963 show was Whitecleat Joyce IV, shown by J. Wilson, Whitecleat, Tankerness. She had previously been the reserve champion at the East Mainland Show.

12 – The County and West Mainland Cheviot champion, 'Woodlands Orcadian', a two-sheer ram, was shown by J. R. Slater, Breck, Orphir.

13 – The Supreme Champion at the 1965 County Show came from Rousay. The champion, also top of the Aberdeen Angus class and winner of the female cup, was a two-year-old A. A. heifer shown by R. R. Johnston, Trumland Farm, Rousay.

14 – A seven-year-old cow, Waterloo Primrose, owned by Mrs A. J. D. Spence, Cavan, Birsay, was Shorthorn champion at both the County and Dounby shows.

15 – This picture shows Mrs Ivy Cromarty, Hools, South Ronaldsay, with her 20-year-old Shetland stallion, Spaniard of Marshwood, which was champion at the County and St Margaret's Hope shows.

16 – A shearling ram, 'Upper Milton Leader', belonging to Ian Moar, West Howe, Birsay, was the champion in the Cheviot section at the County and Dounby shows.

17 – The smallest pony at the East Mainland show is shown here with its owner, Walter Scott, Haulage Contractor, Kirkwall.

18 – At the end of pony judging at the East Mainland Show in 1965, the president of the society, John Tait, Lower Breckquoy, Holm (on right), presented the Royal Highland and Agricultural Society Silver Gilt Long Service Medal to Alex Groundwater, who for over 45 years had worked on the farm of Towerhill, St Ola.

19 – Leaving Orkney in 1963 is Leslie Hodgson, District Officer of the Coastguards in the early '60s. He is seen here receiving a presentation from the staff. Mr Hodgson went to a similar post at Cromer, in East Anglia.

20 – After a storm in 1926 another house was uncovered at the pre-historic site of Skara Brae, in Sandwick. The site was extensively excavated two years later by Professor Gordon Childe, becoming one of Orkney's premier tourist attractions. In the background is Skaill House, itself now open to the public, being visited by increasing numbers annually.

21 – North of Scotland Milk Marketing Board staff of the Cheese Factory enjoy a night out at their dinner dance, held in the Royal Hotel, Kirkwall, in 1963. Standing, left to right: Jack Johnston, Mary Thomson, William Thomson, Danny Pratt, Bell Johnston, John Findlay, Mrs G. Johnston, not known, Mrs Sam Davey, Rene Bain, Gillies Stevenson, David Bain, Clarence Baikie, John Craigie, Rita Spence, Sandy Firth and Mrs Jim Sinclair. Seated, left to right: Mrs D. Pratt, Mrs J. Findlay, Mrs T. Foubister, Tom Foubister, Mrs Marion White, Alister White (Manager), Mrs G. Stevenson, Mrs C. Baikie, Mrs A. Firth and Mrs N. Scollay.

22 – A view of the Kirkwall Pier taken in 1960. Several extensions and reclamation projects have taken place over the years and now a marina is being proposed as part of a waterfront development.

23 – Winners of the Kirkwall Bowling Club shield in 1963 are, left to right: Dave Bews (skip), Peter Leslie, John "Heppy" Sinclair and John "Buddy" Miller.

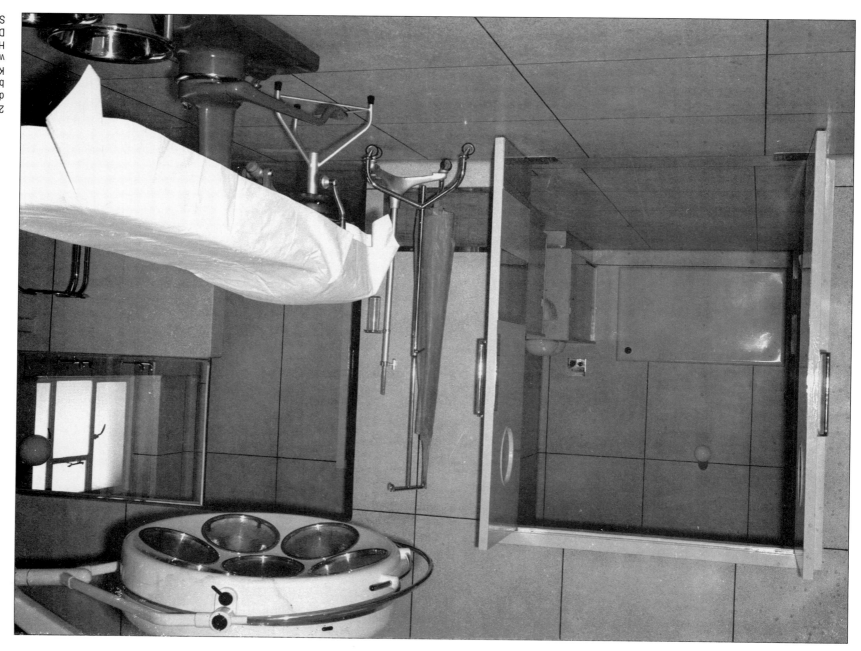

24 – A new outpatients' department and theatre block at Balfour Hospital, Kirkwall, costing £55,000 was opened by Mr T. D. Haddow, Secretary of the Department of Health for Scotland in 1960.

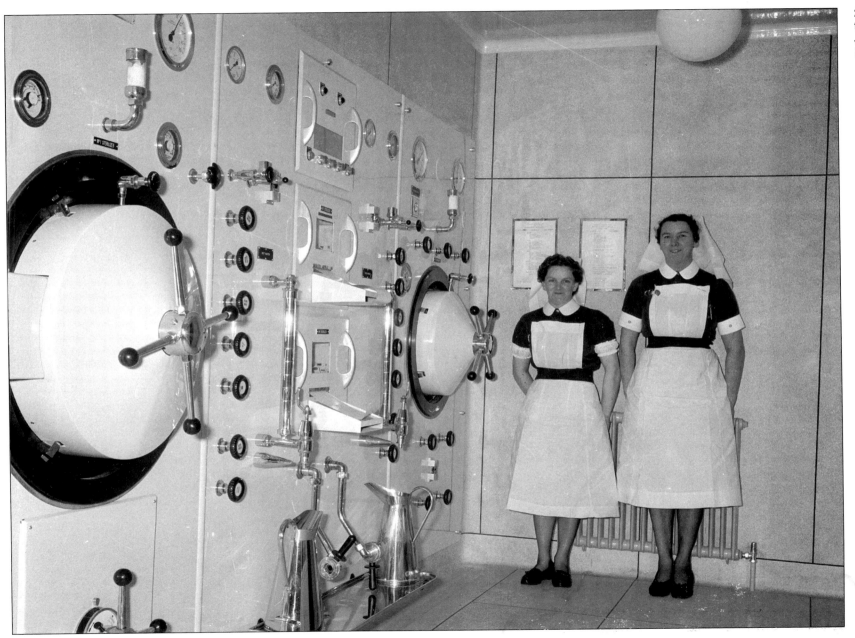

25 – The new operating
theatre staff were Sister
Johanna Rosie (right) and
Nurse Mary Harray.

26 – The East Mainland Young Farmers' Club held their supper and dance and presentation of trophies at the Royal Hotel, Kirkwall. The front row shows the 1962 winners of the Spillers Challenge Trophy, presented to Orkney Association of Young Farmers' Clubs, and awarded to the club gaining most points in stock judging at the annual rally. Front row, left to right: James Taylor; George Eunson, winner of the medal for the highest number of points in the junior section of stock judging and also the overall winner of the junior and senior sections for Orkney and Caithness stock judging; and 14-year-old Tommy Sinclair. Back row, left to right: Leslie Tait, winner of the cup for most points at the root and seed show; Pat Swannie, winner of Royal Highland and Agricultural Society's medal for turnip hoeing. The trophies were presented by Mrs James Laughton Jnr., wife of the club leader.

27 – An assortment of boats are left high and dry at the West Pier, Kirkwall, during an exceptionally low tide in 1966.

28 – A scene from *The Merchant of Venice*, presented by pupils of Kirkwall Grammar School in 1964. From left to right: William Drever, Alan Nixon, Kenny Meason, Alastair Tait, Rognvald Keldie, Evelyn Custer, Jim Meason, Ingrid Thomson, Colin Thomson, Bill Stout. Kneeling: Michael Corsie.

29 – Fursbreck Mashes was a household name in the boom years of egg production in Orkney. Jimmy Rowan, the owner, first came to the county with the Army in 1939 and liked it so much he left his London home to settle here and work as a farm servant. He bought a small croft near Stromness and then Fursbreck in Harray. His business began with a hammer mill operated by a Ferguson tractor which he used to grind the oats. In 1953 he added a small mixer which made the oats into mash. From humble beginnings the business grew, and after ten years Jimmy was supplying 15,000 tons of feed stuff per year. He later opened a new £25,000 plant at the North End in Stromness. He employed 40 men between the two plants. With the decline of the egg industry his business closed in the 1960s. Mr Rowan is seen here on the right showing customers around the mill.

30 – In 1964 a social evening was held in the H.Q. of the 1st Kirkwall Company Boys' Brigade at which a pair of binoculars was presented to Billy Wilson, left, who had taken an active part in the B.B.'s welfare for many years, holding the captaincy in 1961-62-63. The presentation was made by Sgt. John Sim. A bouquet of flowers was presented to Mrs Wilson by Norman Rendall.

31 – After 44 years service as custodian of the Bishop's and Earl's Palaces in Kirkwall, James Hibbert retired in 1964. Mr Hibbert is seen here in the Earl's Palace, standing in front of the banqueting hall fireplace, which has the longest straight arch in Britain.

32 – Kirkwall Toastmasters' Club held a speech-making competition in 1964, open to pupils of Kirkwall Grammar School and Stromness Academy. Of the four boys taking part, James McEwan, William Stout and David Oddie were from Kirkwall Grammar while David Waters came from Stromness Academy. David Waters won first place and received a book token for 25/-. The other three boys received tokens for 20/-. Alastair Scholes, seated, second left, the club president, presented the prizes.

33 – Surplus to requirements! At the end of World War Two, all sorts of left-overs had to be disposed of, including this a stack of unused Churchill Barriers blocks. The woman on the left is Jimmy Sinclair's wife, Annie. On the right is a family friend, Mrs Doreen Pettigrew, and on top of the pile, Major Alan Pettigrew, M.C. Major Pettigrew was Commissioner for the Scottish War Graves, from the late 1940s until the 70s.

34 – The annual visit of Santa Claus to Cumming and Spence, Albert Street, Kirkwall, in 1964 was eagerly awaited by children who turned out in large numbers. Judging by the number on view, the "duffle" coat must have been in fashion at the time.

35 – Shopowner, David G. Spence, Santa and a host of youngsters pose for the photographer in Cumming and Spence's shop.

36 – Members of Kirkwall Water Ski Club begin their 1960 season at the Hatston Slip with one of their members setting off.

37 – The trophy winners of the South Ronaldsay Agricultural Society photographed after the presentation by Mrs M. Brown, wife of the minister, at the Harvest Home held in the Cromarty Hall, St Margaret's Hope, in 1964. Back row, left to right: John Taylor, Thomas Dearness, Marcus Wood, John Scott, John Taylor, Edwin Headley. Front row: James Wishart, John Sinclair, Annie Greig, Metta Mathieson, Nancy McDonald, Andrew Laird.

38 – In glorious summer weather, owners with their pets wait for the judging at the 1965 Congregational Church Fête, in Brandyquoy Park, Kirkwall.

The following three photographs were taken in 1964, in the County Council offices in Broad Street, Kirkwall (now the Tourist Office). The occasion was a local trade fair.

39 – This display shows Orkney farm-style cheese and also the new postal packs introduced at Christmas 1963. The first one was sent to the Lord Mayor of London.

40 – This next picture shows the whisky tasting with Angus Fraser, manager of Scapa Distillery and Harry Russell, local agent for Ambassador whisky.

41 – At another stall we see Sid Watson (on the right) of Scott's Fish Shop, Bridge Street Kirkwall, with his display of lobsters, shellfish etc.

42 – Managers of the Kirkwall banks and their partners enjoy a night out at the 1964 Bankers' Ball, held in the Kirkwall Hotel. Back row, left to right: Mary Reid, Jimmy Cheyne, Margaret Greer, Hamish Reid, not known, Jimmy Greer, Audrey Cheyne. Front row: Iris Swanney, Bill Williamson, Wilma Williamson, Bryce Swanney, Vina Dinwoodie, Norman Williamson.

43 – Not to be outdone, the banking staff and their partners also pose for the camera. Standing, left to right: Duncan Webster, Willie Notman, Anna Hourston and Ian Craig. Seated, left to right: Hilda Park, Jack Walls, Roy Allan, Margaret Sutherland, Colin Leslie, Ruth Douglas, Lyall Johnston, Janet Hicks, Kay Simpson and Kenny Skea.

44 – Some of the Home Fleet in Scapa Bay in 1920. This picture was taken from the Gaitnip shore near to where the HMS *Royal Oak* was sunk by a German U-boat 19 years later, in October, 1939.

45 – Members of the East Mainland Young Farmers' Club pictured in 1964 at Kirkwall airport as they set out to go to Shetland as guests of the Dunrossness Young Farmers' Club. This was the first visit by any Orkney Young Farmers' Club to Shetland.
Left to right: Tommy Sinclair, Dennis Bichan, Tommy Russell, Stanley Ross, David Johnstone, Iris Baillie, Bryan Scott, Kathleen Rendall, Ronnie Baillie, Elizabeth Rendall, Jim Baillie, Rita Pottinger, Norman Smith, Easton Eunson, Angus Drever, Hylton Shearer, Ronnie Laird and Jim Laughton

46 – An outstanding feature of the 1964 Commonwealth Youth Sunday was the presentation of the Royal Humane Society's Testimonial on Parchment to Leslie Johnston, Orley Cottage, St Mary's, Holm, for his bravery in rescuing a drowning woman from Aberdeen Harbour in August 1962. He was a 17-year-old assistant ship's steward at the time.

The presentation was made during the Youth Service in the King Street Church, Kirkwall, by the Lord Lieutenant Col. Robert Scarth of Binscarth, who commended Leslie for his courage and resourcefulness.

The story behind the presentation was that the woman jumped into the dock which was 20 feet deep, with polluted water and flotsam. A lifebuoy was thrown to her but she made no effort to save herself, saying she wanted to be left alone.

Leslie saw what had happened and jumped from his ship on to the pier, removed his outer clothing, and dived in. She did not co-operate at all in her rescue, and it was with difficulty that he managed to get her to the side of the pier, where they were helped from the water.

47 – William (Bill) Harvey, Quoydandy, St Ola, well known cattle and sheep dealer, sold these Shetland ponies to "Bankie" Davidson, Aberdeen's largest pony dealer in the 50s. They were on the first leg of their journey to America.

48 – Five American editors flew to Kirkwall for a lightning three hour visit in 1964. While in Orkney they visited the Highland Park Distillery, took a drive along the shores of Scapa Flow to lunch at Stromness, returned to Kirkwall to inspect a trade exhibition specially laid on for them by Kirkwall Chamber of Commerce, and visited the Cathedral.

Their hosts were Col. H. W. Scarth (Convener), J. Donald Brown (Vice-Convener), Douglas Wood (County Clerk), Lt. Col. Sidney Robertson, Capt. Pat Scott, who showed them round the distillery, Hugh Reid (Orkney Manager B.E.A.) and Gerald Meyer (Editor of *The Orcadian*). The journalists, on a fact-finding visit to the north of Scotland for the tourist trade, also met the provosts of Kirkwall and Stromness.

49 – During a visit to Kirkwall in 1965, and accompanied by his manager and one of his team-mates, Tom MacLaren of the Scottish Kart Racing team demonstrated to a very enthusiastic crowd of spectators at Hatston how to handle a kart. This was one of the earliest go-karts to come to Orkney.

50 – Lieut. Commissioner W. Leed, the Salvation Army's Territorial Commander for Scotland, visited Orkney in 1961. He is seen here after presenting Long Service Awards in Kirkwall. Back row, left to right: Lieut. Trevor Smith (Commissioner's Private Secretary), Capt. Edge and Major Finnie (Commanding Officers), Lieut. Commissioner W. Leed (Territorial Commander, Scotland), Brig. H. Wells (Divisional Commander, North of Scotland). Front row, left to right: Sgt. Major Andrew Stanger (30 years), Madgie Stanger (25 years), Annie Jean Buchan (25 years), Mrs Lily Groat (50 years), William Buchan (25 years), Billy Stanger (10 years), and Gordon Rorie (10 years).

51 – The Ayre Road in Kirkwall after the "big gale" of 1953. For the second time in 12 months, Orkney was battered by hurricane force winds – 125 m.p.h. being recorded at Costa, Evie. Severe damage was reported from all over the county. The West Mainland Mart was destroyed, along with most of the seafront at Kirkwall, where the sea walls were flattened. In Shore Street the public services were all laid bare – water, gas and oil pipes, and electricity cables were exposed. The Ayre Road virtually disappeared altogether and 400 yards of the retaining wall collapsed. Hotels were flooded, chimneys crashed down and houses had to be evacuated. The ss *Earl Thorfinn* was caught in the storm when between Sanday and Stronsay. Captain Hamish Flett tried to get to both islands but was unable to get the ship's head into the wind. Then the steam steering broke and they had to rely on the emergency manual steering gear. They were swept out to the open sea and southward. They eventually arrived outside Aberdeen – 140 miles off course.

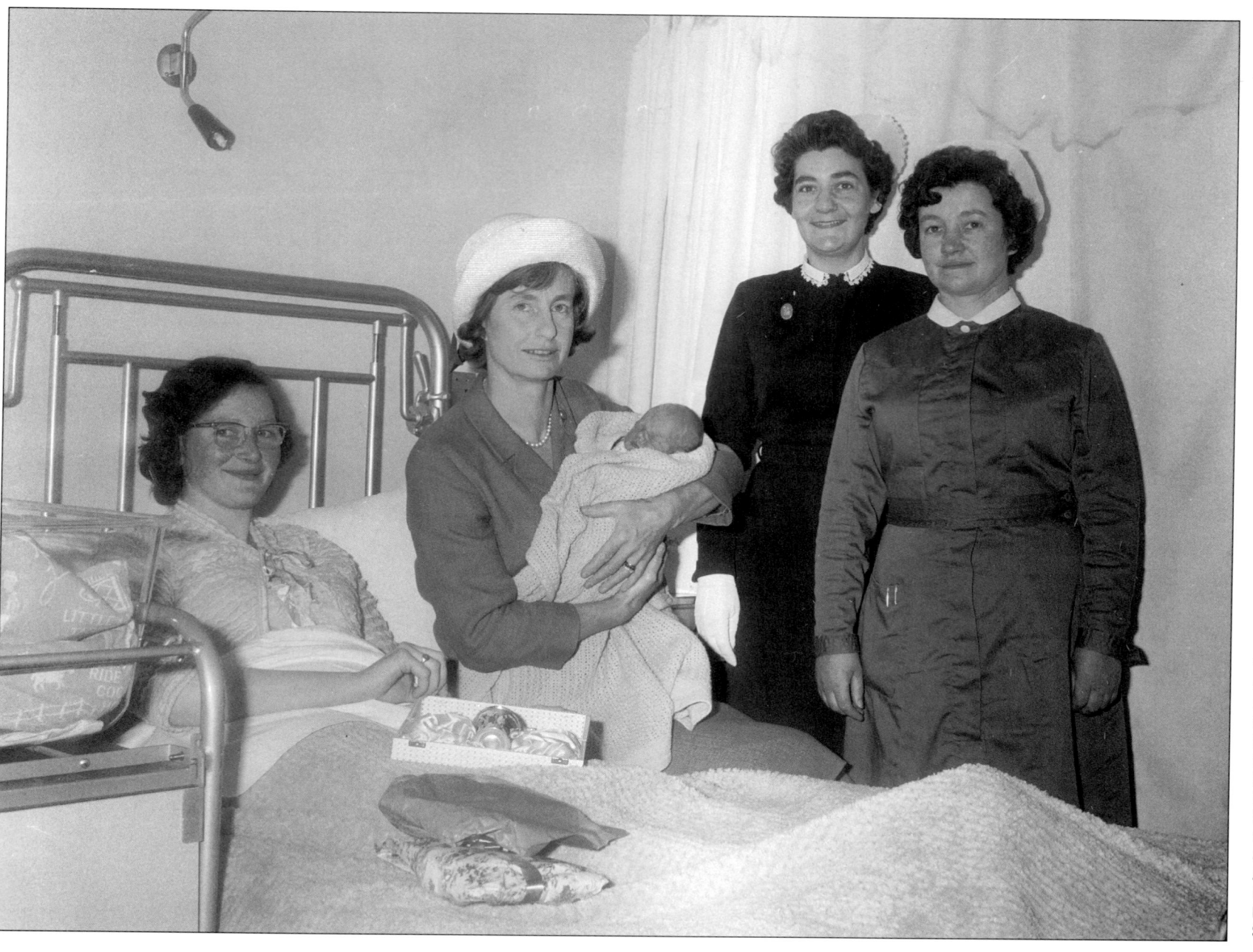

52 – Orkney's new £67,700 Maternity Unit was formally opened at the Balfour Hospital, Kirkwall, in 1966, by Laura Grimond, wife of the M.P, Jo Grimond. She said she had found that the job had already been done for her, by the best possible kind of person to open a maternity wing – namely a baby. Pictured here with Mrs Grimond is baby Stewart Balfour Laing, after she had presented him with a silver christening mug. Also pictured is his mother Moira Laing, Group Matron Margaret Nicolson and Sister Janet Drever.

53 – These smiling mannequins were photographed after the 1964 Young Farmers' Fashion Show held in the Temperance Hall, Kirkwall and Town Hall, Stromness. Ruby Foubister, of the winning Deerness team, is seen holding the trophy. The trophy was commissioned from George Scott by the Orkney County Association for annual competition. Back row, left to right: Lesley Aitken, YF NE Area Chairman, Kathleen Rendall, Betty Foubister, Jennifer Bichan, YF NE Area Organiser, Pat Bichan, Moira Aitken, Elizabeth Rendall, Margaret Rendall and Jack Walls (compere). Front row, left to right: Kathleen Eunson, Chrissie Thomson, Hazel Hepburn, Ruby Foubister, Margaret Skea, Hilda Harrold and Sheena Aitken.

54 – Kirkwall Town Council's new housing scheme, the Quadrant, in 1926. The rent for the new houses was set at 7/6 (37.5 p), and was beyond the means of most working people in the town. The house in the right foreground is Norland, now the St Magnus Cathedral manse.

55 – Some members of the Order of the Eastern Star at their dinner dance in 1964.

56, 57 – School pupils take time out to pose for the photographer during their 1959 Christmas party in the gym hall of Kirkwall Grammar School, now the Orkney Islands Council offices, in School Place.

58 – This sheltered little spot was known as "Quarry Gardens" and was created in the Binscarth plantations in Firth. When Binscarth House was built in 1850 by Robert Scarth – the great, great grandfather of the present owner – the stone was quarried from this nearby site. Later to prevent the disused quarry becoming a general refuse tip, it was decided to create a garden of rosebeds, shrubs, etc and a variety of other flowers, unlikely to survive in Orkney's sea-air. The Quarry Gardens were at their best in the late 1920S but sadly, over subsequent years, they have become overgrown.

59 – The avalanche of cards and mail make Christmas the busiest time of the year for Post Office workers. It was as true in 1963 as it is today and pictured bagging the mail are Bobby Wishart, Donald McKerron and Tommy Heddle at the Kirkwall sorting office.

60 — A group of Deerness Young Farmers, who had been entertaining the residents of Eastbank Hospital, get together with staff to pose for the photographer in 1963.

61 – 1964, a General Election year, and making a presentation to their prospective parliamentary candidate, John Firth, centre, was Bertie Bain, a chartered accountant in Kirkwall. Among those also pictured are Mr Firth's mother Helen, sister, Alison, Bob Bain, George Whittard and Charlie Flett. Mr Firth came second to Jo Grimond, Liberal, in the election.

62 – The draper shop, situated on the corner of Broad Street and Castle Street, belonging to Peace and Low, was destroyed by fire in 1932. The damage at the time was estimated at £5,000. The fire was so intense that the heat cracked the plate glass window of W. T. Sinclair's draper shop across the street (now Lloyds T. S. B.). Davie Oddie, the firemaster, said the fire was so fierce that he feared for the lives of his crew. Jimmy Sinclair and his family were evacuated from their home in Castle Street, which was between the Masonic Hall and the Gas Works (now Castleyards). The building was rebuilt as a draper shop and during the Second World War it was used as a NAAFI, manned by local volunteers. In 1963 the Clydesdale and North Bank opened a branch there.

63 – Isobel Dennison, who was chosen Miss Shapinsay at a dance held by the British Legion in the Shapinsay Hall in 1960.

64 – The new Sanday Secondary School was officially opened in 1964 by Sheriff Harald Leslie, Q.C. Sheriff and Mrs Leslie, along with Robert Mack, Director of Education, James Scott, Chairman of the Education Committee, and several others sailed to Sanday in the morning. The guests were welcomed by the headmaster, John D. Mackay, who showed them over the £114,000 school. Inset: exterior view of the school.

65 – Sanday school pupils in 1964. Left to right: Margaret Work, Mary Sinclair, Ann Alexander, Myra Drever, Sheila Findlay, Vivienne Delday and Elizabeth Brown.

65a – Sanday school pupils in 1964. Back row, left to right: Geordie Peace, George Grieve, Jim Drever, George Simpson, Robbie Wilson. Front row: Tommy Harcus, Andy Lennie, Willie Tulloch, John Goar, Leslie Wilson, Sinclair Simpson, Sandy Drever, Andrew Wilson, Jim Scott and Robert Grieve.

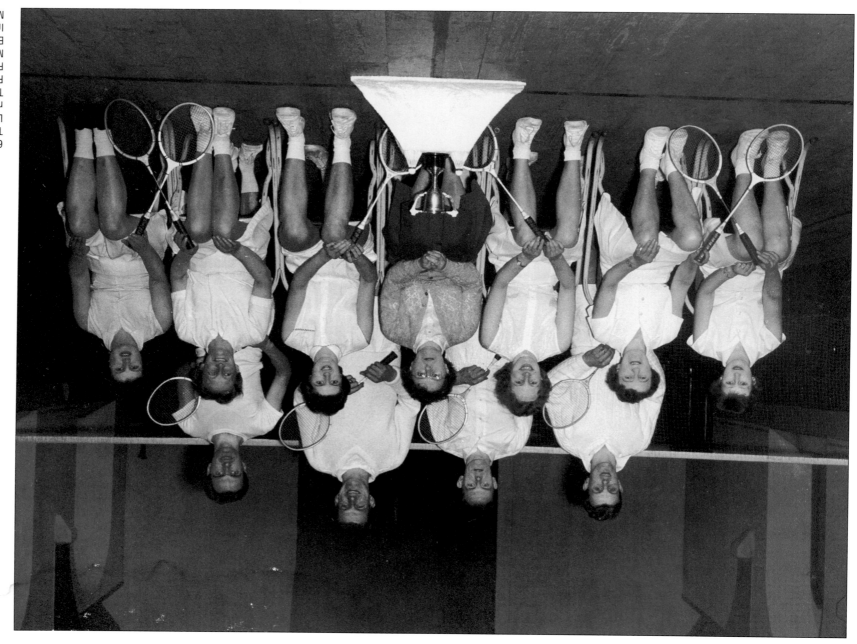

66 – St Magnus Badminton Team, winners of the League Cup in 1960. Back row, left to right: David Tinch, William Spence, John Robertson, John Findlay. Front row, left to right: Moira Tinch, Molly Louttit, Emily Kirkness, J. Pottinger, Irene Kemp, Belle Logie and Marina Maxwell.

67 – A photograph of Bridge Street, Kirkwall, taken in the 1930s showing, on the left, the shop premises of R. Garden. These 200-year-old buildings were the 'hub' of the Garden commercial empire which stretched from Shetland down as far as Ullapool. Born in Aberdeenshire, Robert Garden started a travelling-shop business in Orkney with a horse-drawn van, which was soon followed by more vans, eventually becoming motorised. He also introduced 'shop-boats', firstly using sailing craft and later steamers. Gardens sold all sorts of products: groceries, drapery, footwear, hardware, crockery, feeding stuffs, seeds, fertilisers, oils etc. He had a bakery business, made lemonades etc, and had a weaving business in Junction Road, where the Tower Showroom is now.

68 – In March 1938 a disastrous fire completely gutted the premises of R. Garden in Bridge Street. At the time there were grave concerns in case the fire should spread to the new oil depot at Shore Street. The site of the shop is now a car park for Scarthcentre.

69 – In the 1930s there were a handful of men and a hand-drawn fire appliance to fight fires in Kirkwall. These gallant volunteers are, from left to right: Davie Fox, Jimmy Couper (later burgh surveyor), George Findlater, Davie Oddie (firemaster) and Bob Johnstone.

70 – Thorfinn Football Club held a Beat Festival in the Phoenix Cinema, once a month for four months, during 1964. The concerts, arranged by Ernie Donaldson, were very well attended and the local artistes played to full houses. Some of them are seen here about to fly off "on tour". Back row, left to right: Hazel Groundwater, Jill Leonard, Bertha Flett and Olive Flett. Front row, left to right: Davie Sinclair, Bobby Leslie, Roy Wood, Ivy Corsie, Bobby Corsie, Ian Farquhar and John Schollay.

71 – From the back, left to right: Elizabeth Tait, Anna Davidson, Isobel Herdman, Michael Corsie, Ernie Donaldson, Alan Keldie, Pete Davidson, Colin Omand, Eddie Black and Robert Milne.

72 – The Phoenix Cinema, Kirkwall, was the venue for the 1964 talent contest organised by Thorfinn Football Club. The contestants were competing for the D. G. Spence Jnr. Cup.

73 – The Orkney Federation of the S.W.R.I. held their 1971 Baking Show in the Kirkwall Town Hall. Provost Georgina Leitch, centre, is seen here presenting the trophy for most points to Mrs Lillian Louttit, Lenahowe, Sandwick. Also pictured are, left to right: Sheena Muir, Kathy Hutchison, Peggy Barnett, Mrs Smith, Mary Sinclair and Mary Hourston.

74 – Jo Grimond, MP for Orkney and Shetland, opens the new terminal building at Kirkwall Airport. Mr Grimond, second right, is seen here addressing the assembled company inside the £45,000 building at the Official Opening in April, 1969.

75 – The new airport terminal building, constructed with steel framing and pre-fabricated hardwood timber panels, replaced the old Nissen huts, and was provided by the then Board of Trade, Civil Aviation Department. This building is due to be replaced with a new airport terminal in 2001.

76 – Captain M. S. Clarke, Administrative Officer of the 861 L.A.A. Battery R.A., T.A., receives gifts on his departure in April, 1957, from Major S. P. Robertson, centre. On behalf of his wife and himself he received a silver tea service from the Battery and an Orkney chair from his fellow officers. Captain Clarke was posted to Wales having spent four years in Orkney.

77 – A group of sergeants and their partners pose for the camera at the presentation at Weyland Camp, Kirkwall.

78 – Miss Thorfinn, Elizabeth (Lil) Davey, from Kirkwall, seen here with a line-up of the finalists in the Miss Thorfinn competition at the Cosmo Ballroom in 1960. They are, from left to right: Rhoda MacLean, Mary Thomson, Elizabeth Rendall, Elizabeth Davey, Rita Donaldson, Etta Muir, Ingrid Corsie, Rhoda Liddle

79 – Miss Thorfinn and the other finalists and their partners get together with the officials of Thorfinn Football Club, organisers of the competition.

80 – A golf team from the Northern District, sponsored by Mr W. Walker, visited Orkney in 1963. The four ball foursome, played at Grainbank, ended all square. Back row, left to right: Frazer Urquhart, Jack Mackay, Taylor Bullock, George Donaldson. Front row: Ronnie Gordon, John Grant, William Walker, Donnie Sinclair.

81 – On behalf of the Orkney Golf Club, Mabel Mackintosh (ladies' captain) presented each member of the visiting team with an Orkney rug and tie, to commemorate their visit. Pictured here are the members of the Ladies' Section who looked after the visitors. Back row, left to right: Connie Brodie, Annie Nicolson, Margaret Mackay. Front row: Margaret Sim, Mardi Sclater, Mabel Mackintosh, Margaret Nixon.

82 – Jack Jones, General Secretary of the Transport and General Workers Union (centre, wearing overcoat) paid a visit to Orkney in 1973. Mr Jones is seen here with dockers at Kirkwall Pier.

83 – The opening of the new £30,000 Stenness Community Centre in 1974 was celebrated with a dinner dance. The Opening Ceremony was performed by Col. R. A. A. S. Macrae, Lord Lieutenant of Orkney. At the top table from left to right are: William Muir (vice-chairman), Jean Muir, John Towrie (Secretary of Orkney Council of Social Services), Mona Swannie, James Swannie (chairman of Stenness Community Association), Col. Macrae, Mrs Macrae, Peter Leith (treasurer) and Kathleen Leith.

84 – The Kirkwall Branch of the Royal British Legion organised beauty contests and dances throughout the county at which a "Miss" for the parish was selected by the audience. The climax was a Miss Orkney dance held in the Cosmo Ballroom, Kirkwall, in May each year. The income from these dances went towards building the British Legion Club premises in Kirkwall. This picture shows some of those attending the Miss Rousay dance in 1959.

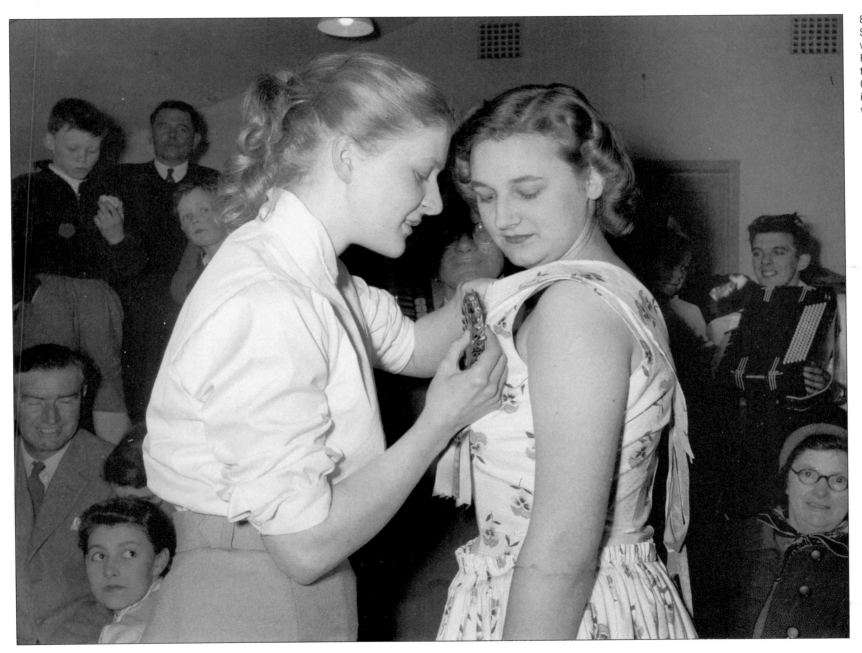

85 – Ruth Miller, Schoolhouse, Wasbister, was chosen to be Miss Rousay, at a dance held in the Rousay Community Centre in 1959. Freda Grieve is seen pinning on the winning rosette.

86 – A group of Royal British Legion stalwarts from the Kirkwall branch pose for the camera. Back row, left to right: D. Richmond, M. MacDonald, T. Payne, J. Duncan, J. Scott, J. Shearer, T. Heddle, J. Urquhart. Middle row: I. Smith, G. Cook, T. Harcus, D. Campbell, D. Foubister, J. Sutherland. Front row: J. I. Harcus, Col. F. Buchanan, T. Kelday, Maj. S. P. Robertson, J. Whyte, J. Horne and J. Craigie.

87 – Mrs Lily Findlay cuts the ribbon at the Official Opening of the extension to the Freemason's Kirkwall Kilwinning Recreation Club in December, 1975.

88 – In 1968 Kirkwall Town Council erected a plaque in St Magnus Cathedral in memory of the historian John Mooney. Mr Mooney was made a Freeman of the City and Royal Burgh of Kirkwall and his son, the Rev. Harald L. Mooney is pictured unveiling the plaque.

89 – In 1968 Mrs Barclay presented Kirkwall Town Council with three chairs in memory of her husband, Rev. William Barclay, who was the minister at the Cathedral for 17 years. The chairs were designed by Dr Stanley Cursiter, carved by Reynold Eunson, and are located in St Rognvald's Chapel. Looking on during Mrs Barclay's speech are, left to right, Bailie A. Mackay, J. D. Brown (County Convener), Provost James Scott, A. Buchan (Town Clerk), Bailie J. B. Gordon and others.

90 – The Civil Defence Division pose for a photograph at their dinner dance, in the Albert Ballroom in 1964.

91 – Some of the machinery inside the Netherbutton transmitting station in 1958. The Holm transmitter gave only limited coverage of T.V. and V.H.F. to Kirkwall and the immediate surroundings when it first opened.
In 1975 a new B.B.C./I.B.A. television station at Keelylang Hill, Firth was opened with a 180 feet high mast and the ability to transmit colour T.V.

92 – The well-known Orkney cattle dealer, D. G. 'Davick' Spence, of Wideford Mains, St Ola, chartered the m.v. *St. Rognvald* to transport over 200 head of cattle to Aberdeen to be sold. It is believed that this was the only occasion where an individual chartered such a boat for this purpose.

93 – The Spence family celebrate with the staffs of their numerous businesses at Christmas in 1960. D. G. Spence Snr, started farming in the farms of Fea and Dalespot, in St Ola. He sold these in 1939 and bought Wideford. In the war years he operated a butcher shop in Kirkwall, and he supplied meat, milk and eggs to the fleet in the Flow. He travelled round the Mainland with his horse and cart, buying eggs from the farms and selling them on to the Navy.

At various times D. G. Spence, his son D. G. Spence Jnr and daughter Mrs Rita Jamieson owned many properties in the county. The Albert and Royal Hotels and the Atholl Cafe; George Rendall, John Sclater's ladies department, J. & J. Smith, The Tree Lane Shop, (drapers); Cumming & Spence, Tree Bakery; John G. Nicolson, (bus operator and garage); Wideford Dairy; and Berstane, Wideford, Mayfield and Hurtiso Farms, and also the burnt out site of the Albert Kinema, which was sold to Lipton's who opened it as Templeton's supermarket. It is now Boots the Chemist. They also supplied contract labour for the Highland Park's peat cutting. Pictured are D. G. Spence, second left, front row, at the Royal Hotel with his staff and their partners.

94 – D. G. Spence Jnr, centre, with Berstane and Wideford Mains staff and partners.

95 – Mrs Rita Jamieson, seated centre, with the Atholl Cafe and the Tree Bakery staff and partners.

96 – Eddie Peace's Band is seen here at a dance in the Royal Hotel, Kirkwall. The band members are, left to right: Mike "Piker" Parkins, Jimmy "Dimmy" Kelday, Sandy Windwick, Jim "Mosh" Marwick, and Eddie Peace. The band played at functions in the 50s and 60s.

97 – After 25 years as head chef at the Kirkwall Hotel, Henryk Zywiecki was presented with a gold watch by Mr Frankland, the area manager of Allied Hotels, Aberdeen. At the presentation in 1972 are back row, left to right: Claude and Maisie George (manager and manageress), Clifford and Jean George, and Henryk's daughter, Frances. Front row, left to right: Mr Frankland, Henryk, and his wife, Joyce. Henryk served a total of 42 years at the hotel.

98 – The Highland Park Distillery was founded in 1798 and is now one of Orkney's foremost tourist attractions. This photograph, taken in 1964, shows men "throwing the mash". This could be so hot that some of the men had to wear clogs, to protect their feet. This part of the process has now been automated. When the work was finished each man got a glass of whisky.

99 – Whisky maturing in the barrel in one of the warehouses in 1964. This warehouse alone holds 6,500 barrels. There are a total of 24 warehouses capable of holding 40,000 to 50,000 casks of whisky.

100 – Art students pause to be photographed in a variety of outrageous outfits during their Charity Week in 1965.

101 – John Sclater's draper shop in Albert Street, Kirkwall, is ready and waiting for the Ba'. John Sclater started the drapery business in 1890 and it continued under his name until 1979. It is now operated as part of the Mackay chain store. Next door neighbours, P. C. Flett Ltd, is now part of the extended Cumming & Spence, bakers, grocers, licensed grocers, etc.

102 – Two Glasgow Rangers Football Club players who were in Orkney are seen here after presenting the Junior Cup to Stromness F.C. in 1961. Back row, left to right: Charlie Clouston, Brian Hourston, Danny Mackay, David Sinclair, George Kirkpatrick, Colin Brown, Ally Park, Jim Sutherland. Front row, left to right: Harold Davis (Rangers F.C.), Erlend Brown, John Anderson, George Berstane (Capt.), Terence Omand, Alan. Muir, Jack Muir, Bill Paterson (Rangers F.C.).

103 – The West Mainland Strathspey and Reel Society with their conductor Isaac Wilson, entertaining the residents of St Peter's House, Stromness, in 1961.

104 – Kirkwall British Legion members and partners enjoy a social evening at the Royal Hotel, Kirkwall, in 1962. Their clubrooms in Great Western Road were opened later that year.

105 – Numerous stacks of Calor Gas cylinders used to be a common sight on Kirkwall pier in the 1960s; either full cylinders which had been shipped to Orkney or empties being returned by sea to be re-filled.
The local agent, John Scott & Miller Ltd had a fleet of vehicles to ferry the bottled gas to and from the firm's store then off Bridge Street (now in the centre of the car park).
Nowadays the gas is transported by articulated trailer from south and taken directly to the firm's depot at Hatston for off loading.

106 – With the 'hairst' safely gathered in, the islanders and friends have a break for the second supper at the Shapinsay Harvest Home in 1958.

107 – Playing at their Harvest Home is the Shapinsay Band: left to right, Davy Towrie, John Nicolson, Billy Mainland and Jim Foubister.

108 – Trophy winners at the Shapinsay Show in August, 1966: left to right, John Hepburn, Tommy Seatter, Tom Groat, John Scott, Alfie Learmonth and Reuben Johnston.

109 – A group of East Mainland Young Farmers try their hand at judging dairy cows at Dalespot, St Ola, in 1963.

110 – In January, 1959 the trawler *George Robb* (left) ran aground in Deersound. Another trawler, the *Viking Monarch*, made an early, but unsuccessful, attempt to pull her clear. After fifteen days on the outcrop of rock, known locally as the South Liddies of Nessie Point, in Tankerness, she was pulled clear by the North Isles boat, ss *Earl Sigurd*. In December of the same year, in a severe gale, the *George Robb* was driven ashore in the Duncansby area. All of the crew were lost.

111 – Jimmy Sinclair photographed these three ladies while on a day trip to Hoy in 1926. They are Miss Aggie Delday, Mrs Jessie Marwick and Miss Ruby Marwick (Mrs Ruby Leslie). The ox was being used to roll a field above Lyness. In former times it was quite common for oxen to be used in the fields and sometimes they would be yoked with a horse for heavy jobs.

112 – Dounby Athletic Football Club won all the cups and trophies they competed for in 1965. This was a remarkable feat, and probably the only time it has happened. Our photograph shows: (l. to r.) Back row: Stewart Spence, Harvey Spence, Harry Flett, Billy Flett, Edric Clouston, Jackie Nicolson, Eric Hutchison, Stanley Hutchison, Bertie Spence. Second row: David Johnstone (president), Tommy Spence (secretary), Jimmy Walls, Stewart Sinclair, Bobby Hutchison, Leslie Flett, Brian Spence, Ian Hutchison, Harold Esson, Frankie Johnston, Jim Stockan (team manager). Third row: David Spence, Tommy Bain, Dennis Leonard, Raymond Stanger, Jackie Walter, Peter Aim, Eoin Macdonald, Jimmy Thomson. Front row: George Wylie, Robert Scott, Alan Flett, Alan Hutchison, Emile Flett, John Stockan, Jockie Wood, Robert Wylie. The club won the following trophies: 'A' team: Brough Cup, Heddle Charity Cup, Challenge Shield. Reserve team: Corsie Cup, Reserve Trophy, Dick Cup. Junior team: Dr Gordon Cup, Junior Cup.

113 – A very heavy overnight fall of snow in 1930 caused problems for shop keepers of Kirkwall's Bridge Street. Council workmen cleared a track in the middle of the street but the merchants were responsible for clearing to their own premises.

114 – During the Seamen's Strike of 1966 (May to July), oil and gas were in very short supply in the county. The mv *Klydon*, belonging to the Dennisons of Shapinsay, and manned by a non union crew, was chartered by S. & J. D. Robertson & Co. Ltd. Empty tanks were loaded at Kirkwall pier and the vessel sailed round to Scapa and then on to Lyness where they were filled from the Royal Naval Establishment oil depot. On returning to Scapa pier they were unloaded by both Shell and Esso. A total of 49,325 gallons of gas oil was transferred to Kirkwall. Supervising the loading at Scapa were John D. M. Robertson, Douglas Laird and Hugh Johnston of Shell.

115 – Two road tankers queue up to receive loads of gas oil from the mv *Klydon*.

116 – Most parishes in Orkney were proud to have raised a volunteer unit during the Second World War. Our picture here shows the Sanday Home Guard. They are from left to right, Back row: William Skea, John Thomson (Eday), David Towrie, John Tulloch, Peter Fotheringham, Peter Harcus, John Muir, Thomas Cursitor, William Skea, James Skea, James Tulloch, Thomas Moodie, Fraser Horne, Malcolm Manson, William Sinclair (Elsness). Second row: Thomas Garrioch, Oliver Meil, William Tulloch, James Skea, Donald Sinclair, Robert Muir, James Skea, James Oliver Alexander, John Swanney, Peter Gray, Billy Skea, George Hay, William Dearness (Whistle), William Dearness (Breckan), John Williamson, William Muir, J. Thomson (Ortie). Third row: Andrew Williamson, George Learmonth, John Bews, John Drever, Andrew Skea, John Tulloch, William Moodie, Rev. Ralston, James Baillie, Walter Garrioch, David Rousay, William Ward, William Rendall, William Tulloch, James Cooper, David Marwick. Front row: Walter Mainland, Andrew Sinclair, Andrew Thomson, John Dearness, Jim Sinclair, Lionel Munro, John Allan, William Muir, David Muir, James Muir, William Towrie, William Williamson, David King, Harry Scott.

117 – This is one of the first pictures taken by Jimmy Sinclair in his new Sinclair's Electric Studio in West Castle Street, Kirkwall. The width of group had to be concentrated to help the illumination of the shot. We see here the Kirkwall Boys' Brigade football team, winners of the Willie Watson Cup, in 1925 or '26. Back row, left to right: A. J. Cromarty, Bill Marwick, Hugh Inkster, J. Mowat, J. Wood. Middle row, left to right:: J. Milne, J. Kemp, G. Sinclair. Front row, left to right: J. Findlay (Titch), A. Marwick, A. Groundwater.

118 – Her Majesty Queen Elizabeth, the Queen Mother, performed the Official Opening of the King George V Memorial Field, on Wednesday, 8th August, 1956. Better known to everyone as "Picky", it has now been incorporated into the Pickaquoy Centre complex. Before the naming ceremony she inspected the Guard of Honour provided by a detachment of Orkney Territorials, the 430 Coastal Regiment, Royal Artillery (T.A.), and the Regimental Pipe Band. Our photo shows Her Majesty being escorted by Major S. P. Robertson and the Lord Lieutenant, Mr P. N. Sutherland Graeme, C.B.E. Provost James Flett welcomed her to the county and presided at the ceremony. The Prayer of Dedication was given by Rev. John M. Rose, minister of the cathedral, and the National Anthem was played by William Buchan, bandmaster of the Salvation Army Band.

119 – During the boom years of the herring fishing industry in Stronsay many hundreds of drifters fished out of the island. We see here some of the fleet of 300 in July 1933. Following the demise of the herring fishing the population went into steep decline. The census figures are as follows: 1921. 1,067; 1931, 953; and in 1951, 641. By the end of the century the number was probably about 350.

120 – This picture, thought to be in 1913, shows a group of Volunteers assembled at the Crafty. The Crafty was the traditional site of the travelling fair which came to Orkney about Lammas each year. The site now forms part of the car park alongside the former Phoenix Cinema in Junction Road, Kirkwall.

121 – A picture of the Earl's Palace in Kirkwall taken from an unfamiliar angle. It appears that someone once had an allotment where the bowling green now nestles and the dyke enclosing Brandyquoy Park has not yet been built.

122 – Preparing to leave Kirkwall in July, 1965 is the Polish ketch *Kismet*. She was on the final stage of a 3,200 mile voyage; a contest sponsored by the Polish Yachting Association.

123 – The four-man crew of the *Kismet* having a break in their epic journey. All four men were involved in naval architecture, the skipper having designed the boat.

124 – The Boys' New Year's Day Ba' of 1957 was thrown up by Pat Gunn, of Edmonton, who was home in Kirkwall after 50 years in Canada. He had been the winner of a Youths' Ba' in 1907, when Men's, Youth's and Boys' Ba's were all played. As a youngster, Pat had been a milk delivery boy, on the Glaitness milk cart, and it was his "duty" when he delivered the milk on "Ba" mornings around 8 a.m. to see that all the likely Uppie players were awake. Pat is seen here waiting for the clock to strike 10 a.m., watched by Davie Ross.

125 – The New Year's Day Boys' Ba' in 1957 went down but the ba' ended up much further out to sea than usual and it was left to the more determined, or foolhardy, to challenge for the coveted trophy. Brian Barnett and a few other bold spirits fought for the honour and were eventually pulled ashore dripping wet.

126 – A cold, tired and dripping wet Brian Barnett with his ba' under his jersey, being carried shoulder high by his supporters.

127 – Once a common sight round the Orkney shores, a Zulu fishing boat gets under way with the crew hoisting her sail. This form of fishing went into decline in the 1920s and 30s and is to be found no more.

128 – In 1959 members of the Kirkwall Junior Dance Club gave a demonstration of ballroom dancing at a Thorfinn F.C. dance in the Cosmo Ballroom, Kirkwall. The dancers were left to right: Lewis and Kathleen Munro; Pat Sangster and Margaret Bews; Michael Cormack and Iris Tulloch. Thorfinn official and M.C. was Jimmy "Dook" Donaldson. Music was provided by the Metronomes, the line-up being: Left to right: Dougie Shearer (drums), Norman Brass (saxophone), Jim Anderson (accordion) and Dougie Cooper (double bass).

129 – Two Clydesdale horses and their handler return home after a hard day of ploughing. Both horses are wearing collars, with a 'hem' attached to the front, and back bands, from which hang chains for supporting the plough and ropes, or 'driving lines.'

130 – The Scapa Seaplane Base was photographed in 1919 by Tom Kent, with Jimmy Sinclair helping to get the photographic equipment to the top of the Scapa cliffs. The Orkney Harbour Authority building now stands on this site.

131 – No wonder Orkney produced such large numbers of eggs when some of the hens were housed in luxurious houses like these.

132 – A Harvey's Bristol Cream sherry tasting evening for the licensed trade at the Kirkwall Hotel in 1962, organised by John Scott & Miller Ltd, Kirkwall, and attended by representatives of Harvey's. Back row, left to right: Jean Heddle, Aly Bruce, Sandy Heddle, Pat Gorie, Ian Argo, Molly Brown, Robert Miller and Claude George. Front row, left to right: Minnie Gorie, Liza Bruce, a Harvey's representative, Maisie George, a Harvey's representative, and Elizabeth Miller.

133 – A group of Sandwick and Stromness artistes, entertaining the senior citizens of the parish in 1974, had a surprise visit from Jimmy Shand, who joined in the music making. The famous entertainer was a personal friend of the Sinclair family and frequently performed at benefit events or for charity.

134 – Members of Orkney Cadet Regiment, Army Cadet Force, pictured in the Drill Hall, Weyland Park, Kirkwall, during an inspection by Brigadier R. A. Phayre, D.S.O., R.A., in 1952. The regiment was made up of units from Harray (H), Kirkwall (K) and Stromness (S). The officers and warrant officer seated in the second row are from left to right: 2/Lieut. L. I. Rendall (K); Lieut. J. Wishart (S); Lieut. E. Hamer, O.C. (S); Captain J. W. Shearer, Commanding Officer of Orkney Cadet Regiment; Lieut. Col. F. Buchanan, Secretary, County Cadet Committee and Interim Secretary, Territorial & Auxiliary Forces Association; Brigadier R. A. Phayre, D.S.O., R.A., Commanding 105 Coast Artillery Brigade; Lieut. Col. B. L. Swanney, Commanding Officer, 430 Coast Regiment R.A. (T.A.); Lieut. J. Sweeney, O.C., (K); 2/Lieut. N. Sinclair (K); and B.S.M. D. Towers (H). Cadet personnel are: Back row: Sergeant F. Park (S); Cadet L. Blance, L/Bdr. F. Croy and L/Bdr. B. Donaldson (K); Cadet J. Arcus (S); Cadet D. Bews (K); Cadet A. Merriman (H); Cadets L. Hadden and W. Fraser (K); Cadet S. Shearer (H); and Bdr. A. Turmeau (S). Third row: Cadets P. McKinlay, J. Scollie, S. Yule, R. Rendall; L/Bdr. F. Rorie; Cadets. J. Heddle, L. Macdonald; L/Bdr. E. Sommerville (all K); L/Bdr. J. Towers (H); and Cadet I. Cameron (K). Front row: Cadets G. Harrison, R. Johnstone, K. Donaldson, C. Swanney and D. Rosie (all K).

135 – In 1967 Miss Jeanie Johnston achieved 50 years service to local government and she is pictured here receiving a portable radio from Kirkwall Provost James Scott, on behalf of the council and her colleagues. In the picture, from left to right are: Helen Nicolson (deputy town clerk), Ken Ross, Jeanie Johnston, James Couper (burgh surveyor), Provost Scott, Andrew Buchan (town clerk), Bill MacKintosh (clerk of works), Elizabeth Rees, Angus Findlater and Helen MacLean.

137 – This picture of the Firth Tennis Club 1934-35 was taken at the tennis court next to the Pomona Inn, Finstown. From left to right are, back row: Lizzie Paterson, John Thomson, Herbert Jolly, Dave Flett, Jim Yorston, Robert Learmonth, Jim Manson, Tom Davie, George Lamont. Middle row: Mina Harcus, Mabel Keldie, Iris Laird, Maggie Linklater, Ivy Scarth, Mary Heddle, Emily Keldie, Nurse D. Green, Emily Yorston, Feebie Tait, Katie Thompson, Mona Matches. Sitting on ground: Colin Keldie, Barrie Firth, Jean Heddle, John Tulloch, Bob Firth.

138 – Over a hundred members of Kirkwall Townswomen's Guild pose for this photo taken in the 1950s. Yet, less than 50 years later, in 1998, the guild had to be disbanded due to lack of support.

139 – The Air Training Corps in the KGS playground several years after they were formed in the early 1940s. Back row, left to right: Sinclair Ross, Bill Moss, Ronald Kemp, not known, John Tulloch, Jackie Miller, David Eunson, David Moss. Middle row: Jim Work, John Muir, Joe Walker, Colin MacGillivray, Norman Cooper, Ernie Hourston, John Dearness, Allie Seater, Jim Scott, William Donaldson, Dave Logie. Front row: Norman Peace, Charles Findlater, Bob Firth, John Goodall, Wilson, Ronald Cheyne, not known.

140 – There was considerable interest among Orcadians in 1930 when this seaplane landed in Kirkwall Bay and moored off the West Pier. To keep the aircraft safe over night a set of wheels were attached and it was hauled up a ramp near to the Ayre Hotel. In the background is one of the Earl steam ships which served the North Isles.

141/142 – This flying boat caused great excitement in Kirkwall in the early 1930s when it flew in unexpectedly. It stayed for several days and it is understood that it was on a training exercise for young RAF pilots.

143 – Overlooking the Loch of Harray, is Merkister, the former home of Orcadian novelist, playwright, journalist, essayist and poet, Eric Linklater. When Eric and his wife Marjorie left Orkney in 1947, they sold the house to a Mr Watson. The house was subsequently sold to Mr and Mrs Jim Smith in 1950. It was their family home for six years. It was not lived in for two years until Mr and Mrs Tough bought it and turned it into an hotel in 1958. Today the Merkister Hotel is recognised as one of Scotland's finest fishing hotels.

144 – In May, 1956, the British European Airways 47-seat Viscount V701 aircraft started service to Kirkwall. The original 701 Viscounts, with Dart 505 engines, were being converted during 1955 to V701A's with Dart 50b engines, enabling the operating weight to be raised by 3,000 lbs. It was the summer of 1962 before the 66-seat Viscount arrived.

Acknowledgement

My sincere thanks to everyone who helped me compile Images in Time Volume 3. Every little scrap of information has been priceless and although I cannot begin to name everyone individually, I do want to make special mention of the kind and helpful staff at The Orkney Library, and Archive Department.

Thank you everyone; I am in your debt.

NORMAN F. SINCLAIR
October, 2000

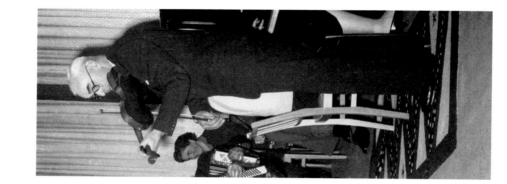

Index